A Treasury of

New Testament Stories

The Stories of Jesus, Mary, The Good Samaritan,
Zacchaeus, and Many Others

This book
is for

_____

From

_____

A Treasury of
New Testament STORIES

The Stories of Jesus, Mary, The Good Samaritan,
Zacchaeus, and Many Others

ideals children's books™
Nashville, Tennessee

ISBN 0-8249-5494-7

Published by Ideals Children's Books
An imprint of Ideals Publications
A division of Guideposts
535 Metroplex Drive, Suite 250
Nashville, Tennessee 37211
www.idealsbooks.com

Printed and bound in Italy by LEGO

Color separations by Precision Color Graphics, Franklin, Wisconsin

Designed by Jenny Eber Hancock

10 9 8 7 6 5 4 3 2 1

Contents

The Story of Jesus

by Patricia A. Pingry

Illustrated by Rebecca Thornburgh

Jesus

is the Son

of God.

He loves

us very much.

We

celebrate

Jesus's

birthday

at Christmas.

On Easter,

we remember

that Jesus

gave his

life

for us.

We read in

the Bible

about Jesus

and his

twelve

disciples.

Jesus

was very kind.

He said,

"Love one

another as

I love you."

One day, some children came up to Jesus. His friends said,

"Go away.

Jesus is tired."

But Jesus

said, "Let the

little children

come to me.

All people

should

have the faith

of a little child."

Jesus

performed

many

miracles.

He made sick

people well.

One day, Jesus was preaching. The people got very hungry.

One little boy had five rolls and two fish for his lunch.

The boy gave it to Jesus to share. Jesus fed **five thousand people** with the boy's lunch.

Jesus

promised

that he would

be with us

forever.

When we

pray,

we ask Jesus

to help us.

32

We love

Jesus,

because

he first

loved us.

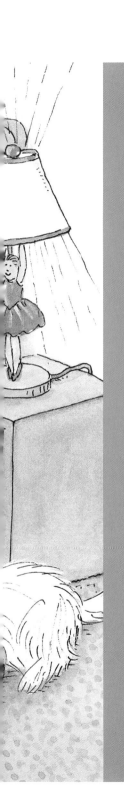

The Story of The Lord's Prayer

by Patricia A. Pingry

Illustrated by Elaine Garvin

Did you know

that you can talk to

God

just as you talk

to your

mom or dad?

You can learn

to pray the prayer

Jesus taught us.

We call it the

Lord's Prayer.

"Our Father,
which art in heaven . . ."

I have a father on earth,

but you, God,

are my

heavenly father.

Samuel Jason Cathy Susan Eric Jillian Martha Thomas

42

"Hallowed be
thy name . . ."

I will respect
your name, God.

"Thy kingdom come . . ."

I pray that

the whole world

will love you, God.

Puppet Center

Cathy

Susan

45

"Thy will be done . . ."

I will do what

you, God,

want me to do.

"In earth,
as it is in heaven."

I will listen to you

always like

the angels do

in heaven.

49

"Give us this day
our daily bread."

Thank you,

God, for my food

each day.

"And forgive us our debts,
as we forgive our debtors."

I will forgive other children

who have hurt me.

God, forgive me

when I hurt others.

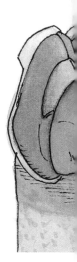

53

54

"Lead us not
into temptation . . ."

Please, God,

don't even let me

see something

that makes me

want to do wrong.

"But deliver us
from evil . . ."

God, keep me safe.

57

"For thine is the kingdom,
and the power,
and the glory, for ever."

God, you are more powerful

than anyone or anything.

Be with me always.

Amen.

The Story of the Good Samaritan

by Patricia A. Pingry

Illustrated by Stacy Venturi-Pickett

Do you know

how to be

a good

neighbor?

Are you

kind

and

helpful

to others,

even if they

are different?

Jesus

told us a story

about being a

good neighbor.

One day a man

was walking

down a road.

Suddenly some men

jumped

out at him.

They took his money

and clothes.

They ran away.

A

priest

came walking

down the road.

He saw the hurt man.

But the priest

crossed to the

other side of the road.

Later,

a Levite

came down the road.

When he saw the man,

he crossed

the road too.

A man from

another country, a

Samaritan,

came walking down

the road.

Nobody

liked Samaritans.

They were different.

The Samaritan

saw the man

lying beside the road

and knelt beside him.

The Samaritan

wiped

the man's face,

gave him water,

and helped him

on his donkey.

The Samaritan

led the donkey

to an inn

and asked for a room.

He helped the man

into a clean, cool bed.

The good Samaritan

called for a

doctor.

Then he left money

for more care

and went on his way.

Jesus wants us

to be

good

neighbors,

just like the

good Samaritan . . .

even to those

who are

different.

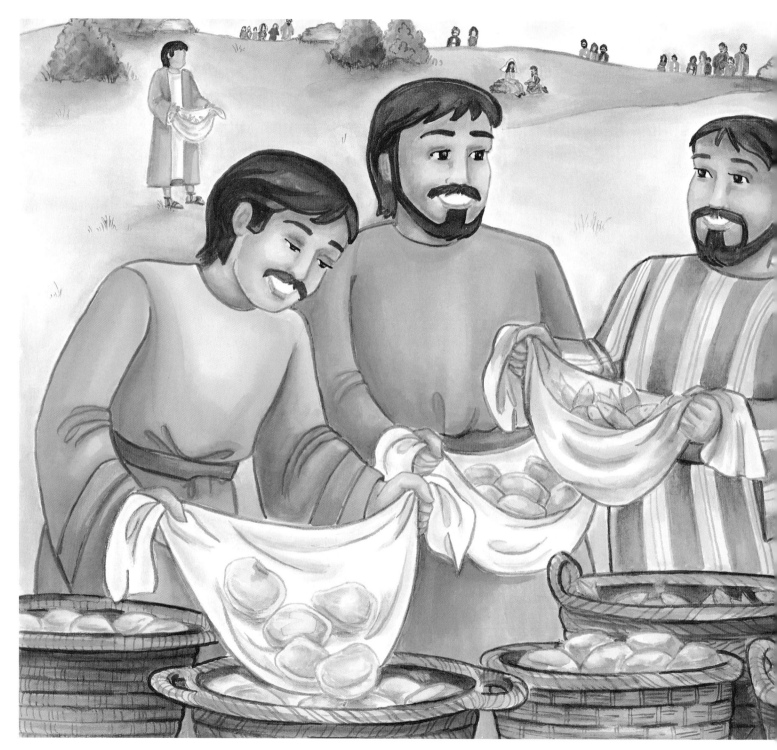

The Story of the Loaves & Fishes

by Patricia A. Pingry

Illustrated by Stacy Venturi-Pickett

Jesus taught

people about

God.

One day, Jesus

was teaching

more than

five thousand

people.

Some people

sat on the grass.

Others stood

side by side.

All were

very still and

listened

to Jesus's words.

When the sun

began to go down,

some people

felt

hungry.

Philip, one of

Jesus's disciples, said,

"Jesus,

tell the people to

leave

so they can go

eat supper."

But Jesus said,

"Give them

some

food

to eat."

"But," Philip answered,

"we don't have

enough

money

to buy food for

five thousand people!"

Another disciple,

Andrew, spoke up.

"One little boy

brought his lunch.

He will

share his

five rolls

and

two fish."

The little boy

gave his

lunch

to Jesus.

Jesus gave

thanks

to God

for the food.

"Pass this
food around,"

Jesus said.

The disciples thought,

"Five loaves and two fish

will not feed

all of these people."

But they passed

around the food.

Men wrapped their bread around their fish.

Women chewed the bread and then the fish.

Children nibbled bread only.

They ate and talked and ate and ate.

Finally the people sighed, "We are stuffed!"

The disciples picked up the leftovers. They filled **twelve baskets** with fish and bread.

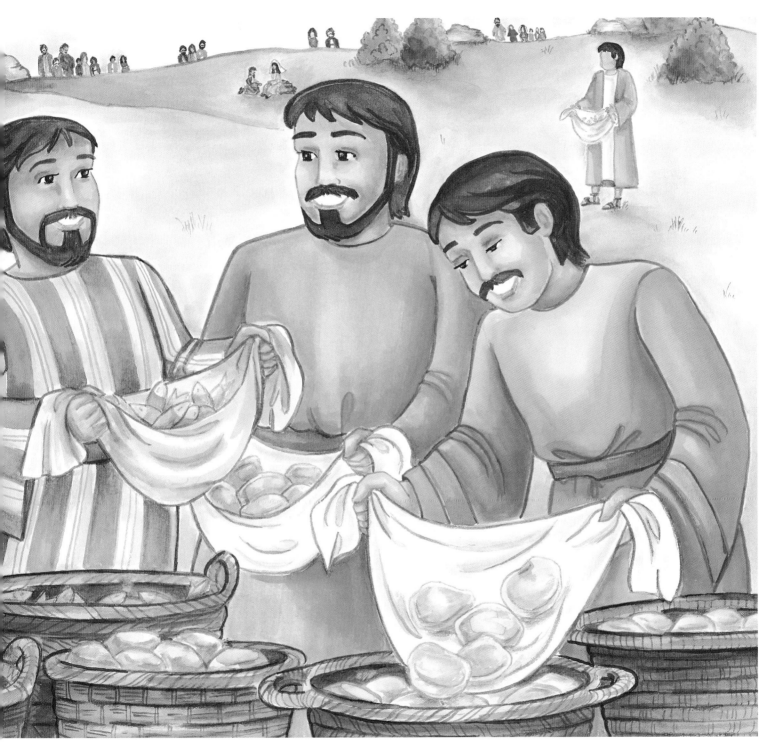

Then the

people said,

"Jesus

fed us with

only two fish

and five loaves.

He is truly

God's Son."

The Story of Zacchaeus

by Patricia A. Pingry

Illustrated by Stacy Venturi-Pickett

Have you ever

done something

you're sorry you did?

The Bible tells about

Zacchaeus,

who was sorry

and was

forgiven.

Zaccheus was a

tax collector.

But he took

more money

than the people

owed for tax.

One day

Zaccaeus

heard that

Jesus

was coming

to town.

Zacchaeus wanted

to see him.

When Zacchaeus

went to see Jesus,

there were so many

people that

Zacchaeus

couldn't

see.

Zacchaeus

jumped up to see.

He

peeked

between people.

But he could not

see Jesus.

So Zaccheus

climbed

a tall

tree.

Now he could see

over the people.

Jesus saw Zacchaeus

in the tree.

"Come down,

Zacchaeus,"

Jesus called.

"I want to go

home with you."

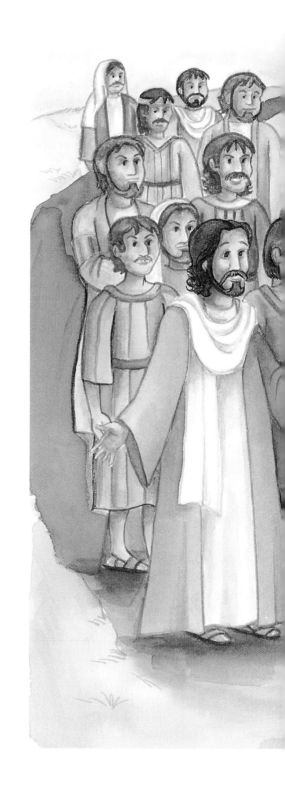

The people gasped.

They shook their heads.

They wagged their fingers.

"Zacchaeus is a

thief,"

they said.

"He takes more money

than we owe!"

Jesus said,

"I have come to

save

all people,

even thieves."

So Zacchaeus

came down.

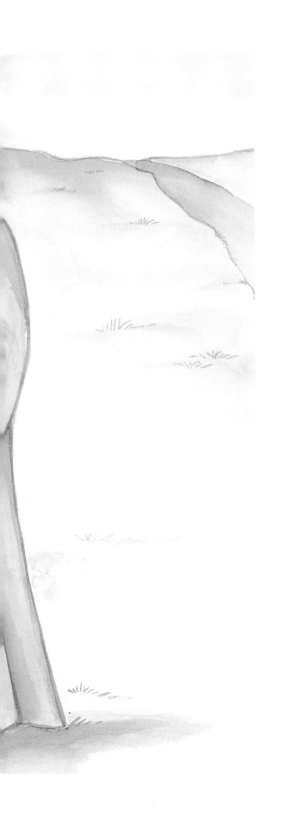

Zacchaeus

was ashamed

that he had

taken the

money.

He said,

"I will give money

to the poor,

even more than I took."

Jesus said,

"Zacchaeus, today

you are

saved

because your heart

has changed."

Jesus loved

Zacchaeus.

And Jesus loves us, too,

no matter what.

138

The Story of Mary

by Patricia A. Pingry

Illustrated by Stacy Venturi-Pickett

A long time ago,

a girl named

Mary

lived in the town of

Nazareth

in Judea.

One day an angel, named

Gabriel,

visited Mary.

"You will be the mother

of a very special baby,"

said Gabriel.

"The baby will be

God's Son.

His name will be Jesus."

After the angel left,

Mary ran to tell

her cousin

Elizabeth.

Elizabeth was

also going to

have a baby.

Then Mary went to tell

Joseph

about the baby.

Joseph would be Jesus's

earthly father.

Then the ruler

of the country ordered,

"You must go

to your parents' birthplace

and be counted."

Mary and Joseph

had to go to

Bethlehem

to be counted.

Mary rode a

donkey.

Joseph

walked.

The trip took

many days.

There were many people

in Bethlehem

and there was

no room

for Mary and Joseph.

There was

no bed

for Mary

in Bethlehem.

154

So Joseph made a bed

for Mary in a

stable.

That night,

God's Son was born.

Mary called him

Jesus.

Angels announced

the birth of

Mary's son to

shepherds.

The angels said,

"You will find the babe

lying in a

manger."

The shepherds ran

to see Mary's baby.

God sent a

star

to mark the place

where Jesus lay.

The star led wise men

to the manger.

They brought

Baby Jesus

gold,

frankincense,

and

myrrh.

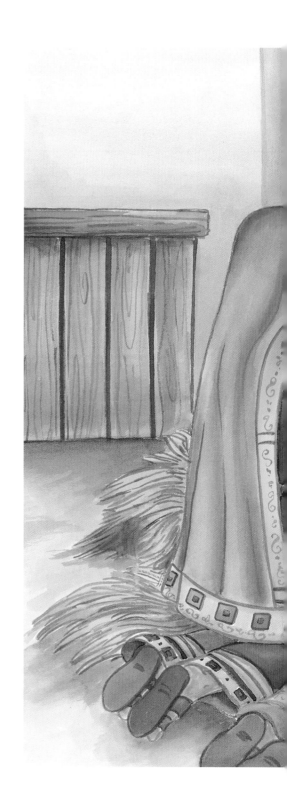

After the visitors left,

Mary held her

baby close.

She knew

that the angel

had been right.

Jesus was

very special.

The Story of Christmas

by Patricia A. Pingry

Illustrated by Lorraine Wells

Do you know

why we give gifts at

Christmas?

We give presents

because it is

Jesus's

birthday.

168

Long ago,

an angel told

Mary

she would have a

baby

named Jesus.

Mary and her husband, Joseph,

were very

happy.

They had a lot to do

to get ready for the baby.

First, they

had to take

a long trip

to Bethlehem.

Mary rode a

donkey;

Joseph walked.

When they

got to

Bethlehem,

many people

were there.

Mary

and

Joseph

were very tired,

but there was

no place for

them to stay.

177

They slept on a

bed of hay in a

stable

with a cow

and the donkey.

179

180

That night,

Baby Jesus

was born.

Angels

told the

shepherds,

"Jesus is born!

You will find him

lying in a

manger."

183

Wise men

followed

a star

to the stable

and

Baby Jesus.

They all

brought

Baby Jesus

presents

because

they loved him.

We give

gifts at Christmas

to show our

love

and to say,

"Happy birthday,
Baby Jesus."

191

THE STORY OF JESUS
The Books of Matthew, Mark, Luke, and John

THE STORY OF THE LORD'S PRAYER
Matthew 6:5-13

THE STORY OF THE GOOD SAMARITAN
Luke 10:30-37

THE STORY OF THE LOAVES AND FISHES
John 6:1-14

THE STORY OF ZACCHAEUS
Luke 19:1-10

THE STORY OF MARY
Luke 1:26-56; 2:1-19

THE STORY OF CHRISTMAS
Luke 2:1-19; Matthew 2:1-12